The Joyful Mysteries

AN ILLUSTRATED ROSARY BOOK FOR KIDS AND THEIR FAMILIES

THE ILLUMINATED ROSARY
Revised Edition

TEXT BY JERRY WINDLEY-DAOUST
ORIGINAL CONCEPT BY MARK DAOUST

For an introduction to praying the rosary with this book, see page 92.

The Canticle of Mary (Magnificat)

My soul proclaims the greatness of the Lord;
my spirit rejoices in God my Savior
for he has looked with favor on his lowly servant.
From this day all generations will call me blessed;
the Almighty has done great things for me
and holy is his name.
He has mercy on those who fear him
in every generation.
He has shown the strength of his arm,
and has scattered the proud in their conceit.
He has cast down the mighty from their thrones,
and has lifted up the lowly.
He has filled the hungry with good things,
and the rich he has sent away empty.
He has come to the help of his servant Israel
for he has remembered his promise of mercy,
the promise he made to our fathers,
to Abraham and his children forever.

In the name of the Father,
and of the Son, and of the Holy Spirit.
Amen.

I believe
in God, the Father almighty,
Creator of heaven and earth,
and in Jesus Christ,
his only Son, our Lord,
who was conceived by the Holy Spirit,
born of the Virgin Mary,
suffered under Pontius Pilate,
was crucified, died and was buried;
he descended into hell;
on the third day he rose again from the dead;
he ascended into heaven,
and is seated at the right hand
of God the Father almighty;
from there he will come to judge
the living and the dead.

I believe in the Holy Spirit,
the holy catholic Church,
the communion of saints,
the forgiveness of sins,
the resurrection of the body,
and life everlasting.
Amen.

Our Father
who art in heaven,
hallowed be thy name.
Thy kingdom come.
Thy will be done on earth,
as it is in heaven.

Give us this day our daily bread,
and forgive us our trespasses,
as we forgive those
who trespass against us,
and lead us not into temptation,
but deliver us from evil.

Amen.

FOR FAITH

Hail, Mary, full of grace, the Lord is with thee.
Blessed art thou among women,
and blessed is the fruit of thy womb, Jesus.
Holy Mary, Mother of God, pray for us sinners,
now and at the hour of our death. *Amen.*

FOR HOPE

Hail, Mary, full of grace, the Lord is with thee.
Blessed art thou among women,
and blessed is the fruit of thy womb, Jesus.
Holy Mary, Mother of God, pray for us sinners,
now and at the hour of our death. *Amen.*

FOR CHARITY

Hail, Mary, full of grace, the Lord is with thee.
Blessed art thou among women,
and blessed is the fruit of thy womb, Jesus.
Holy Mary, Mother of God, pray for us sinners,
now and at the hour of our death. *Amen.*

Glory be to the Father,
and to the Son, and to the Holy Spirit;
as it was in the beginning, is now, and ever shall be,
world without end. *Amen.*

The Annunciation

God sent the angel Gabriel to announce
to Mary that God was with her in a special way,
and that she would become
the mother of Jesus: the Son of God
and Savior of the world.

At first, Mary wondered how this could be.
But the angel said,
"Nothing is impossible with God."

Mary said to the angel, "I am God's servant;
let it be done to me as you say."

INTENTIONS

Our Father
who art in heaven,
hallowed be thy name.
Thy kingdom come.
Thy will be done on earth,
as it is in heaven.

Give us this day our daily bread,
and forgive us our trespasses,
as we forgive those
who trespass against us,
and lead us not into temptation,
but deliver us from evil.

Amen.

AVE·GRA
TIA·PEENA·

The Annunciation

Hail, Mary, full of grace, the Lord is with thee.
Blessed art thou among women,
and blessed is the fruit of thy womb, Jesus.

Holy Mary, Mother of God, pray for us sinners,
now and at the hour of our death. *Amen.*

Hail, Mary, full of grace, the Lord is with thee.
Blessed art thou among women,
and blessed is the fruit of thy womb, Jesus.

Holy Mary, Mother of God, pray for us sinners,
now and at the hour of our death. *Amen.*

The Annunciation

Hail, Mary, full of grace, the Lord is with thee.
Blessed art thou among women,
and blessed is the fruit of thy womb, Jesus.

Holy Mary, Mother of God, pray for us sinners,
now and at the hour of our death. *Amen.*

Hail, Mary, full of grace, the Lord is with thee.
Blessed art thou among women,
and blessed is the fruit of thy womb, Jesus.

Holy Mary, Mother of God, pray for us sinners,
now and at the hour of our death. *Amen.*

The Annunciation

Hail, Mary, full of grace, the Lord is with thee.
Blessed art thou among women,
and blessed is the fruit of thy womb, Jesus.

Holy Mary, Mother of God, pray for us sinners,
now and at the hour of our death. *Amen.*

Hail, Mary, full of grace, the Lord is with thee.
Blessed art thou among women,
and blessed is the fruit of thy womb, Jesus.

Holy Mary, Mother of God, pray for us sinners,
now and at the hour of our death. *Amen.*

The Annunciation

Hail, Mary, full of grace, the Lord is with thee.
Blessed art thou among women,
and blessed is the fruit of thy womb, Jesus.

Holy Mary, Mother of God, pray for us sinners,
now and at the hour of our death. *Amen.*

Hail, Mary, full of grace, the Lord is with thee.
Blessed art thou among women,
and blessed is the fruit of thy womb, Jesus.

Holy Mary, Mother of God, pray for us sinners,
now and at the hour of our death. *Amen.*

The Annunciation

Hail, Mary, full of grace, the Lord is with thee.
Blessed art thou among women,
and blessed is the fruit of thy womb, Jesus.

Holy Mary, Mother of God, pray for us sinners,
now and at the hour of our death. *Amen.*

Hail, Mary, full of grace, the Lord is with thee.
Blessed art thou among women,
and blessed is the fruit of thy womb, Jesus.

Holy Mary, Mother of God, pray for us sinners,
now and at the hour of our death. *Amen.*

The Annunciation

Glory be to the Father,
  and to the Son, and to the Holy Spirit;
as it was in the beginning, is now,
and ever shall be, world without end.
  Amen.

O my Jesus, forgive us our sins,
save us from the fires of hell;
lead all souls to heaven, especially
those in most need of thy mercy.

The Visitation

The angel Gabriel told Mary
that her kinswoman, Elizabeth,
was going to give birth to a son
who would announce the coming of Jesus

Mary went to visit Elizabeth,
and the child within Elizabeth leaped for joy.

"Blessed art you among women,"
Elizabeth exclaimed,
"and blessed is the fruit of your womb."

And Mary praised God:
"My soul magnifies the Lord,
and my spirit rejoices in God my Savior!"

Mary stayed with Elizabeth for
three months before returning home.

INTENTIONS

Rembrandt 1640.

Our Father
who art in heaven,
hallowed be thy name.
Thy kingdom come.
Thy will be done on earth,
as it is in heaven.

Give us this day our daily bread,
and forgive us our trespasses,
as we forgive those
who trespass against us,
and lead us not into temptation,
but deliver us from evil.

Amen.

This is the PLACE of our DELight and rest.
St. Jane de Chantal

The Visitation

Hail, Mary, full of grace, the Lord is with thee.
Blessed art thou among women,
and blessed is the fruit of thy womb, Jesus.

Holy Mary, Mother of God, pray for us sinners,
now and at the hour of our death. *Amen.*

Hail, Mary, full of grace, the Lord is with thee.
Blessed art thou among women,
and blessed is the fruit of thy womb, Jesus.

Holy Mary, Mother of God, pray for us sinners,
now and at the hour of our death. *Amen.*

The Visitation

Hail, Mary, full of grace, the Lord is with thee.
Blessed art thou among women,
and blessed is the fruit of thy womb, Jesus.

Holy Mary, Mother of God, pray for us sinners,
now and at the hour of our death. *Amen.*

Hail, Mary, full of grace, the Lord is with thee.
Blessed art thou among women,
and blessed is the fruit of thy womb, Jesus.

Holy Mary, Mother of God, pray for us sinners,
now and at the hour of our death. *Amen.*

The Visitation

Hail, Mary, full of grace, the Lord is with thee.
Blessed art thou among women,
and blessed is the fruit of thy womb, Jesus.

Holy Mary, Mother of God, pray for us sinners,
now and at the hour of our death. *Amen.*

Hail, Mary, full of grace, the Lord is with thee.
Blessed art thou among women,
and blessed is the fruit of thy womb, Jesus.

Holy Mary, Mother of God, pray for us sinners,
now and at the hour of our death. *Amen.*

The Visitation

Hail, Mary, full of grace, the Lord is with thee.
Blessed art thou among women,
and blessed is the fruit of thy womb, Jesus.

Holy Mary, Mother of God, pray for us sinners,
now and at the hour of our death. *Amen.*

Hail, Mary, full of grace, the Lord is with thee.
Blessed art thou among women,
and blessed is the fruit of thy womb, Jesus.

Holy Mary, Mother of God, pray for us sinners,
now and at the hour of our death. *Amen.*

The Visitation

Hail, Mary, full of grace, the Lord is with thee.
Blessed art thou among women,
and blessed is the fruit of thy womb, Jesus.

Holy Mary, Mother of God, pray for us sinners,
now and at the hour of our death. *Amen.*

Hail, Mary, full of grace, the Lord is with thee.
Blessed art thou among women,
and blessed is the fruit of thy womb, Jesus.

Holy Mary, Mother of God, pray for us sinners,
now and at the hour of our death. *Amen.*

The Visitation

Glory be to the Father,
and to the Son, and to the Holy Spirit;
as it was in the beginning, is now,
and ever shall be, world without end.
Amen.

O my Jesus, forgive us our sins,
save us from the fires of hell;
lead all souls to heaven, especially
those in most need of thy mercy.

The Nativity

Mary and her husband Joseph
traveled to Bethlehem.
Jesus was born in a stable there,
because there was nowhere else
for them to stay.

Wise men from far away learned of Jesus's birth,
and brought him gifts
of gold, frankincense, and myrrh.

And angels appeared to some shepherds
watching over their sheep.

"Do not be afraid," one of the angels said.
"I am bringing you good news
of great joy for all the people:
to you is born this day a Savior,
who is the Messiah, the Lord."

INTENTIONS

Our Father
who art in heaven,
hallowed be thy name.
Thy kingdom come.
Thy will be done on earth,
as it is in heaven.

Give us this day our daily bread,
and forgive us our trespasses,
as we forgive those
who trespass against us,
and lead us not into temptation,
but deliver us from evil.

Amen.

The Nativity

Hail, Mary, full of grace, the Lord is with thee.
Blessed art thou among women,
and blessed is the fruit of thy womb, Jesus.

Holy Mary, Mother of God, pray for us sinners,
now and at the hour of our death. *Amen.*

Hail, Mary, full of grace, the Lord is with thee.
Blessed art thou among women,
and blessed is the fruit of thy womb, Jesus.

Holy Mary, Mother of God, pray for us sinners,
now and at the hour of our death. *Amen.*

The Nativity

Hail, Mary, full of grace, the Lord is with thee.
Blessed art thou among women,
and blessed is the fruit of thy womb, Jesus.

Holy Mary, Mother of God, pray for us sinners,
now and at the hour of our death. *Amen.*

Hail, Mary, full of grace, the Lord is with thee.
Blessed art thou among women,
and blessed is the fruit of thy womb, Jesus.

Holy Mary, Mother of God, pray for us sinners,
now and at the hour of our death. *Amen.*

The Nativity

Hail, Mary, full of grace, the Lord is with thee.
Blessed art thou among women,
and blessed is the fruit of thy womb, Jesus.

Holy Mary, Mother of God, pray for us sinners,
now and at the hour of our death. *Amen.*

Hail, Mary, full of grace, the Lord is with thee.
Blessed art thou among women,
and blessed is the fruit of thy womb, Jesus.

Holy Mary, Mother of God, pray for us sinners,
now and at the hour of our death. *Amen.*

The Nativity

Hail, Mary, full of grace, the Lord is with thee.
Blessed art thou among women,
and blessed is the fruit of thy womb, Jesus.

Holy Mary, Mother of God, pray for us sinners,
now and at the hour of our death. *Amen.*

Hail, Mary, full of grace, the Lord is with thee.
Blessed art thou among women,
and blessed is the fruit of thy womb, Jesus.

Holy Mary, Mother of God, pray for us sinners,
now and at the hour of our death. *Amen.*

The Nativity

Hail, Mary, full of grace, the Lord is with thee.
Blessed art thou among women,
and blessed is the fruit of thy womb, Jesus.

Holy Mary, Mother of God, pray for us sinners,
now and at the hour of our death. *Amen.*

Hail, Mary, full of grace, the Lord is with thee.
Blessed art thou among women,
and blessed is the fruit of thy womb, Jesus.

Holy Mary, Mother of God, pray for us sinners,
now and at the hour of our death. *Amen.*

Glory be to the Father,
and to the Son, and to the Holy Spirit;
as it was in the beginning, is now,
and ever shall be, world without end.
Amen.

O my Jesus, forgive us our sins,
save us from the fires of hell;
lead all souls to heaven, especially
those in most need of thy mercy.

The Presentation

Mary and Joseph took the baby Jesus
to the Temple in Jerusalem
to present him to the Lord.

Now, in the Temple that day
was a holy man named Simeon
and a prophet named Anna.
Simeon and Anna had been waiting
many years for the Messiah,
the one sent by God
to bring salvation to Israel.

When Simeon and Anna saw Jesus,
they praised God,
for they knew that Jesus was the one
who would fulfill all of God's promises;
they rejoiced for the coming of God's salvation.

INTENTIONS

Our Father
who art in heaven,
hallowed be thy name.
Thy kingdom come.
Thy will be done on earth,
as it is in heaven.

Give us this day our daily bread,
and forgive us our trespasses,
as we forgive those
who trespass against us,
and lead us not into temptation,
but deliver us from evil.

Amen.

The Presentation

Hail, Mary, full of grace, the Lord is with thee.
Blessed art thou among women,
and blessed is the fruit of thy womb, Jesus.

Holy Mary, Mother of God, pray for us sinners,
now and at the hour of our death. *Amen.*

Hail, Mary, full of grace, the Lord is with thee.
Blessed art thou among women,
and blessed is the fruit of thy womb, Jesus.

Holy Mary, Mother of God, pray for us sinners,
now and at the hour of our death. *Amen.*

The Presentation

Hail, Mary, full of grace, the Lord is with thee.
Blessed art thou among women,
and blessed is the fruit of thy womb, Jesus.

Holy Mary, Mother of God, pray for us sinners,
now and at the hour of our death. *Amen.*

Hail, Mary, full of grace, the Lord is with thee.
Blessed art thou among women,
and blessed is the fruit of thy womb, Jesus.

Holy Mary, Mother of God, pray for us sinners,
now and at the hour of our death. *Amen.*

The Presentation

Hail, Mary, full of grace, the Lord is with thee.
Blessed art thou among women,
and blessed is the fruit of thy womb, Jesus.

Holy Mary, Mother of God, pray for us sinners,
now and at the hour of our death. *Amen.*

Hail, Mary, full of grace, the Lord is with thee.
Blessed art thou among women,
and blessed is the fruit of thy womb, Jesus.

Holy Mary, Mother of God, pray for us sinners,
now and at the hour of our death. *Amen.*

The Presentation

Hail, Mary, full of grace, the Lord is with thee.
Blessed art thou among women,
and blessed is the fruit of thy womb, Jesus.

Holy Mary, Mother of God, pray for us sinners,
now and at the hour of our death. *Amen.*

Hail, Mary, full of grace, the Lord is with thee.
Blessed art thou among women,
and blessed is the fruit of thy womb, Jesus.

Holy Mary, Mother of God, pray for us sinners,
now and at the hour of our death. *Amen.*

The Presentation

Hail, Mary, full of grace, the Lord is with thee.
Blessed art thou among women,
and blessed is the fruit of thy womb, Jesus.

Holy Mary, Mother of God, pray for us sinners,
now and at the hour of our death. *Amen.*

Hail, Mary, full of grace, the Lord is with thee.
Blessed art thou among women,
and blessed is the fruit of thy womb, Jesus.

Holy Mary, Mother of God, pray for us sinners,
now and at the hour of our death. *Amen.*

The Presentation

Glory be to the Father,
and to the Son, and to the Holy Spirit;
as it was in the beginning, is now,
and ever shall be, world without end.
Amen.

O my Jesus, forgive us our sins,
save us from the fires of hell;
lead all souls to heaven, especially
those in most need of thy mercy.

The Finding of Jesus in the Temple

When Jesus was twelve years old,
he traveled with Mary and Joseph
to Jerusalem to celebrate the Passover.
But when it was time to return home,
Jesus stayed in Jerusalem.

Mary and Joseph searched for three days
before finding him in the Temple,
listening to the teachers and asking them questions.

His mother said:
"Child, why have you treated us like this?
We have been searching for you in great anxiety!"

"Why were you searching for me?"
Jesus replied. "Did you not know
that I must be in my Father's house?"

Then Jesus returned to Nazareth
with his parents,
where he grew in wisdom;
and Mary treasured these things in her heart.

INTENTIONS

Our Father
who art in heaven,
hallowed be thy name.
Thy kingdom come.
Thy will be done on earth,
as it is in heaven.

Give us this day our daily bread,
and forgive us our trespasses,
as we forgive those
who trespass against us,
and lead us not into temptation,
but deliver us from evil.

Amen.

The Finding of Jesus in the Temple

Hail, Mary, full of grace, the Lord is with thee.
Blessed art thou among women,
and blessed is the fruit of thy womb, Jesus.

Holy Mary, Mother of God, pray for us sinners,
now and at the hour of our death. *Amen.*

Hail, Mary, full of grace, the Lord is with thee.
Blessed art thou among women,
and blessed is the fruit of thy womb, Jesus.

Holy Mary, Mother of God, pray for us sinners,
now and at the hour of our death. *Amen.*

The Finding of Jesus in the Temple

Hail, Mary, full of grace, the Lord is with thee.
Blessed art thou among women,
and blessed is the fruit of thy womb, Jesus.

Holy Mary, Mother of God, pray for us sinners,
now and at the hour of our death. *Amen.*

Hail, Mary, full of grace, the Lord is with thee.
Blessed art thou among women,
and blessed is the fruit of thy womb, Jesus.

Holy Mary, Mother of God, pray for us sinners,
now and at the hour of our death. *Amen.*

The Finding of Jesus in the Temple

Hail, Mary, full of grace, the Lord is with thee.
Blessed art thou among women,
and blessed is the fruit of thy womb, Jesus.

Holy Mary, Mother of God, pray for us sinners,
now and at the hour of our death. *Amen.*

Hail, Mary, full of grace, the Lord is with thee.
Blessed art thou among women,
and blessed is the fruit of thy womb, Jesus.

Holy Mary, Mother of God, pray for us sinners,
now and at the hour of our death. *Amen.*

The Finding of Jesus in the Temple

Hail, Mary, full of grace, the Lord is with thee.
Blessed art thou among women,
and blessed is the fruit of thy womb, Jesus.

Holy Mary, Mother of God, pray for us sinners,
now and at the hour of our death. *Amen.*

Hail, Mary, full of grace, the Lord is with thee.
Blessed art thou among women,
and blessed is the fruit of thy womb, Jesus.

Holy Mary, Mother of God, pray for us sinners,
now and at the hour of our death. *Amen.*

The Finding of Jesus in the Temple

Hail, Mary, full of grace, the Lord is with thee.
Blessed art thou among women,
and blessed is the fruit of thy womb, Jesus.

Holy Mary, Mother of God, pray for us sinners,
now and at the hour of our death. *Amen.*

Hail, Mary, full of grace, the Lord is with thee.
Blessed art thou among women,
and blessed is the fruit of thy womb, Jesus.

Holy Mary, Mother of God, pray for us sinners,
now and at the hour of our death. *Amen.*

The Finding of Jesus in the Temple

Glory be to the Father,
and to the Son, and to the Holy Spirit;
as it was in the beginning, is now,
and ever shall be, world without end.
Amen.

O my Jesus, forgive us our sins,
save us from the fires of hell;
lead all souls to heaven, especially
those in most need of thy mercy.

Hail, holy Queen,
Mother of Mercy:
our life, our sweetness and our hope.
To thee do we cry,
poor banished children of Eve;
To thee do we send up our sighs,
mourning and weeping in this valley of tears.
Turn then, most gracious advocate,
thine eyes of mercy toward us;
and after this our exile,
show unto us the blessed fruit of thy womb, Jesus.
O clement, O loving,
O sweet Virgin Mary.

V. Pray for us, O holy Mother of God.

R. That we may be made worthy of the
promises of Christ.

In the name of the Father, and of the Son,
and of the Holy Spirit. *Amen.*

Art Credits

All works are in the public domain, except as otherwise noted.

Cover: Donaldson Brothers, *Raphael's Madonna*, 1898. Art reproduction of Raphael's Sistine Madonna (1513–1514). Licensed under public domain via Library of Congress Prints and Photographs Division.

Title page: Bartolomé Esteban Murillo, *The Holy Children with a Shell*, 1670.

Title page, 23, 39, 55, 71, 87, back cover: Jessica Connelly, *Joyful Mysteries Rose Wreath*, 2018. All rights reserved. Used with permission. Artist website: https://telos.design

2: Jen Norton, *Canticle of Mary*, 2014. © Jen Norton. Used with permission. Artist website: jennortonartstudio.com

5: Hans Memling, *Music-Making Angels*, 1440s.

7: Lorenzo Lotto, *Madonna of the Rosary*, 1539.

The Annunciation

8–9: Bardi Barth, Mysteries of the Rosary: *Annunciation*. Copyright © HERBRONNEN vzw; all rights reserved. Used with permission. Artist website: www.bradi-barth.org

10–11: Luis Lagarto, *The Annunciation*, 1610.

12–13: Leonardo da Vinci, *The Annunciation*, c. 1472–1475.

14: Fra Angelico, *The Annunciation*, 1425–1428.

15: Apollonio di Giovanni, *The Annunciation*, 15th century.

16: Philippe de Champaigne, *The Annunciation*, c. 1644.

17: El Greco, *The Annunciation*, 1596–1600.

18: Henry Ossawa Tanner, *The Annunciation*, 1898.

19: Agnolo Bronzino, *Virgin of the Annunciation*, 1540–1545.

20: Simone Martini and Lippo Memmi, *The Annunciation*, 1333.

21: Guido of Siena, *Annunciation*, 1262–1279.

22: Daniel Bonnell, *The Annunciation II*, 2017. All rights reserved. Used with permission. Artist website: bonnellart.com

The Visitation

24–25: Rembrandt van Rijn, *The Visitation*, 1640. Photography licensed from Detroit Institute of Art (Detroit)/Bridgeman Images.

26–27: Brother Michael "Mickey" O'Neill McGrath, O.S.F.S., *The Windsock Visitation*. All rights reserved. Used with permission. Artist website: bromickeymcgrath.com

28: Master of Spes Nostra, *Memorial Tablet*, 1500.

29: Unknown, untitled, 1410. Wool, linen, silk. Museum für Angewandte Kunst (Frankfurt).

30: Vicente Masip, *The Visitation*, 1540–1545.

31: Piero di Cosimo, *The Visitation with Saint Nicholas and Saint Anthony Abbot*, c. 1490.

32: Jacopo Pontormo, *Visitation*, 1528–1529.

33: Unknown, untitled; from a polyptych panel in the chapel of Tyrol Castle, Merano, Italy. Licensed from Adobe Stock.

34: Raphael, *The Visitation*, 1590.

35: Frans Francken, *The Visitation of Virgin Mary to Elizabeth*, 1618. Licensed from Adobe Stock.

36: Jerónimo Ezquerra, *The Visitation*, early 18th century.

37: Philippe De Champaigne, *The Visitation*, 1643–48.

38: Federico Barocci, *Visitation*, c. 1590–1610. Licensed from Adobe Stock.

The Nativity

40–41: Fritz Eichenberg, *Christmas, 1954*, 1954. Art © The Fritz Eichenberg Trust / Licensed by VAGA, New York, NY. Used with permission.

42–43: Thomas Cole, *The Angel Appearing to the Shepherds*, 1834.

44: Workshop of Giorgione, *The Adoration of the Shepherds*, 1510.

45: Matthias Stom, *The Adoration of the Shepherds*, 1635–1637.

46: Anthony van Dyck, *Virgin and Child with Saint Catherine of Alexandria*, 1630.

47: Guido Reni, *St. Joseph with the Infant Jesus*, 1620.

48: Fra Angelico and Fra Filippo Lippi, *The Adoration of the Magi*, 1440–1460.

49: Cigoli, *The Adoration of the Shepherds with Saint Catherine of Alexandria*, 1599. Metropolitan Museum of Art.

50: Giotto di Bondone, *The Adoration of the Magi*, 1320. Metropolitan Museum of Art.

51: Peter Paul Rubens, *The Adoration of the Magi*, 1628–1629.

52–53: Edward Burne-Jones, *The Adoration of the Magi*, 1904. Wikimedia.

54: Jacob Jordaens the Elder, *Flight of the Holy Family Into Egypt*, 1647.

The Presentation

56–57: Philippe de Champaigne, *The Presentation in the Temple*, 1802.

58–59: Andrei N. Mironov, *Saint Simeon with the Christ Child*, 2014. Licensed under CC BY-SA 4.0. Artist website: artmiro.ru

60–61: Pietro Perugino, *Presentation in Temple*, 15th century. Licensed from Adobe Stock.

62: Fra Angelico, *The Presentation of Jesus in the Temple*, 1440–1442.

63: Jean Bourdichon, *The Presentation in the Temple*, 1498–1499.

64: James Tissot, *The Presentation of Jesus in the Temple*, 1886–1894.

65: Alvaro Pirez, *The Presentation in the Temple*, 1430. Metropolitan Museum of Art.

66: Stefan Lochner, *Presentation of Christ in the Temple*, 1447.

67: Rembrandt van Rijn, *Simeon's Song of Praise*, 1631.

68: Rembrandt van Rijn, *Simeon in the Temple*, 1627–1628.

69: Gian Domenico Facchina, *The Presentation of Jesus in the Temple*, 1900. Licensed from Adobe Stock.

70: Jacob Jordaens, *The Presentation in the Temple*, 17th century.

The Finding in the Temple

72–73: Bénédite de la Roncière, *Jesus among the Teachers*, c. 1973. © VIE DE JÉSUS MAFA 24, rue du Maréchal Joffre 78000 Versailles, FRANCE. Used with permission. ww.jesusmafa.com

74–75: Max Liebermann, *Jesus in the Temple*, 1879.

76–77: Vasili Dmitrievich Polenov, *Among the Teachers*, 1896. State Tretyakov Gallery (Moscow). Used with permission.

78: Ludovico Mazzolino, *The Twelve-Year-Old Jesus Teaching in the Temple*, 1524.

79: Simon Bening, *The Dispute in the Temple*, 1525–1530.

80: Orazio Borgianni, *Jesus Amongst the Doctors*, 1610.

81: Bernardino Luini, *Christ Among the Doctors*, 1515–1530.

82: Gian Domenico Facchina, *The Finding of Jesus in the Temple*, c. 1900. Photo by Fr. Lawrence Lew, O.P. Used with permission.

83: Unknown, *Christ in the Temple*. Stained glass in Immaculate Heart of Mary (Hayes, Middlesex, UK). Photo by G. Licence. Used with permission.

84–85: William Holman Hunt, *The Finding of the Saviour in the Temple*, 1860.

86: James Tissot, *Jesus Found in the Temple*, 1886–1894.

88: Bartolomé Esteban Murillo, *Virgin and Child in Glory*, 1673.

Back cover: Unknown artist, untitled; from a polyptych panel in the chapel of Tyrol Castle, Merano, Italy. Licensed from Adobe Stock.

How to Pray the Rosary with This Book

WELCOME to THE ILLUMINATED ROSARY, a way of praying the rosary more meditatively with the help of sacred art. THE ILLUMINATED ROSARY was first developed for families with young children, but has proven popular with young and old alike.

Using THE ILLUMINATED ROSARY is simple:

- The *full text* of every prayer is printed in order, so that young readers might learn to pray the rosary without distraction.
- Each mystery is introduced with a brief, *child-friendly reading* loosely based on the Scriptures. In the rosary, a mystery is an episode in the life of Christ or Mary that unfolds God's plan of salvation. After reading about each mystery, you will be prompted to state the *intentions* for which you are praying.
- The *sacred art* on every spread is meant to aid prayerful meditation. As you pray each decade, remember the words of Pope Paul VI: "By its nature the recitation of the Rosary calls for a quiet rhythm and a lingering pace, helping the individual to meditate on the mysteries of the Lord's life..." (Pope Paul VI, Marialis Cultus #47).
- The roses around the text of each Hail Mary serve as *rosary beads*, helping kids keep track of where they are in the decade.

Here are some practical suggestions for praying THE ILLUMINATED ROSARY with children:

- *Keep it short* at first, saying one decade of the rosary in a single sitting. *Try praying antiphonally*: one group or person says the first half of each prayer, and the other group or person says the second half.
- Optionally, *ask your family for intentions* for each decade. For whom or for what do you wish to offer the prayers of the decade?
- After you are finished praying, *ask your children what thoughts or feelings* they had as they meditated on each mystery. Which artwork "spoke" to them most? How might the Holy Spirit have been speaking to them through their meditation?

You may find some of the artwork in these pages not to your personal taste. That is natural; but to get the most out of your meditation, try viewing these images sympathetically. Let the vision of the artist challenge you: Why would the artist paint the mystery as he or she did? What does it reveal to the artist and others who have appreciated it? However you use THE ILLUMINATED ROSARY, may praying with it lead you closer to the heart of Jesus through the heart of his mother; and may your own heart be filled with awe, reverence, and wonder.

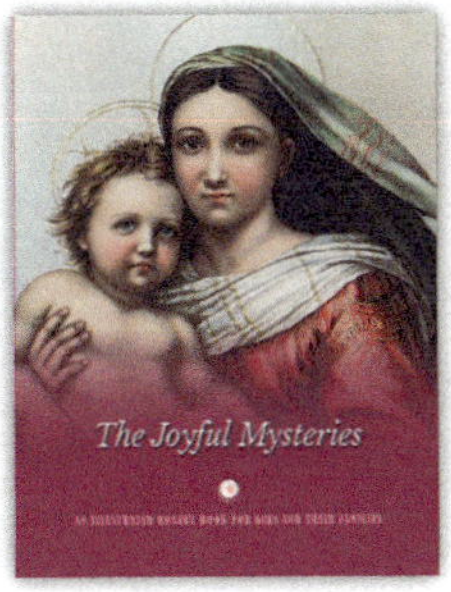

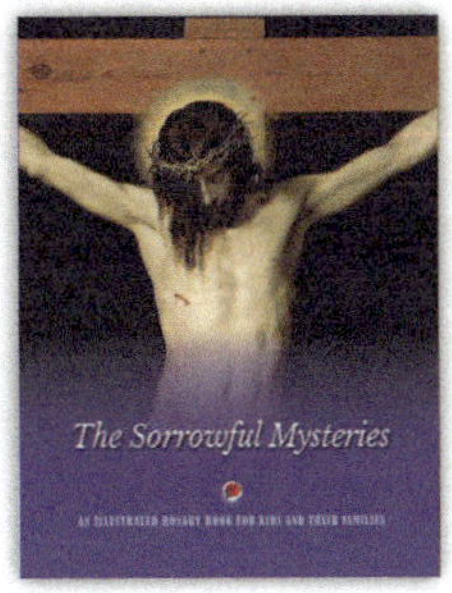

Dedicated to the memory of Norman G. Daoust.

Nihil obstat:
Rev. Timothy Hall, *Censor librorum*

Imprimatur:
†Most Rev. John M. Quinn, Bishop of Winona
October 25, 2014

The imprimatur is an official declaration that a book or pamphlet is free of doctrinal or moral error. No implication is contained therein that those who have granted the imprimatur agree with the contents, opinions, or statements expressed.

The Illuminated Rosary, Revised Edition
The Joyful Mysteries
An Illustrated Rosary Book for Kids and The ir Families

31 30 29 28 27 26   5 6 7 8 9 10 11

ISBN: 978-1-68192-510-3 (Inventory No. T2399)

JUVENILE NONFICTION / Religion / Devotional & Prayer
JUVENILE NONFICTION / Religion / Christianity / Christian Life
RELIGION / Christianity / Catholic

LCCN: 2019939990

Book design and build by Steve Nagel.
Acknowledgments assistance by Sara Dethloff.
Proofing by Karen Carter.

See art credits, page 90, for copyright statements
pertaining to individual artworks.

Our Sunday Visitor Publishing
www.osv.com